Successfully Dealing with Difficult People in a week

BRIAN SALTER
NAOMI LANGFORD-WOOD

Successfully
Dealing with
Difficult People
in a week

BRIAN SALTER
NAOMI LANGFORD-WOOD

LEARNING RESOURCES
CENTRE
Havering College
of Further and Higher Education

Hodder & Stoughton

A MEMBER OF THE HODDER HEADLINE GROUP

Orders: please contact Bookpoint Ltd, 39 Milton Park, Abingdon, Oxon OX14 4TD. Telephone: (44) 01235 400414, Fax: (44) 01235 400454. Lines are open from 9.00 - 6.00, Monday to Saturday, with a 24 hour message answering service. Email address: orders@bookpoint.co.uk

British Library Cataloguing in Publication Data
A catalogue record for this title is available from The British Library

ISBN 0 340 72076 X

First published 1998
Impression number   10 9 8 7 6 5 4
Year   2004 2003 2002 2001 2000

Cover photo from Tony Stone Images.

Typeset by Multiplex Techniques Ltd, St Mary Cray, Kent.
Printed in Great Britain for Hodder & Stoughton Educational, a division of Hodder Headline Plc, 338 Euston Road, London NW1 3BH by Cox & Wyman Ltd, Reading, Berks.

C O N T E N T S

There can be nothing more demoralising than having to deal with difficult people. You get to meet them everywhere – in bus queues and supermarkets, on the motorways and at airports, and in a whole variety of areas where stress can lead quite 'normal' people to behave rudely, impatiently or emotionally; or even a devastating combination of all three.

Many difficult people do not even realise that they are behaving badly; others, on the other hand, do so systematically because:

- it makes us feel uncomfortable, anxious, upset or angry
- it instils a feeling of negativity in us
- it coerces us into doing things we would rather not do
- it prevents us from doing what we would like to do
- it makes us feel guilty if we do not go along with their wishes

In short, it makes them feel they have the upper hand.

In the workplace, perhaps more so than anywhere else, learning to handle difficult people can result in getting the best out of them, and by a natural extension, the best out of us, whether they are fellow workers, aggressive managers, customers or suppliers.

Learning about what it is that may make them behave in the way that they do can reduce our stress levels, and allow us to operate much more effectively, whilst at the same time ensuring that we become much more valued as team members amongst our peers.

■ I N T R O D U C T I O N ■

This book is written as a step-by-step guide to encourage managers to stop for a moment, to look for the warning signs in people's behavioural patterns and to analyse what it is that makes them tick. Every day considers a different aspect, and by the end of the week, the following topics will have been covered:

Sunday	Understanding yourself
Monday	Different styles of behaviour
Tuesday	Coping with different problem people
Wednesday	Managing conflict situations
Thursday	Basic communications skills and body language
Friday	How to say 'no' and deal with difficult clients
Saturday	You're in control now

After all, as difficult people rarely see themselves as difficult, they are most unlikely to think that they should read this book.

Although we have referred to 'he' throughout this text, we are not trying to be sexist – as can be seen from the co-authorship of this book!

Understanding yourself

To start at the beginning, we should perhaps define what we mean by the term 'difficult people'. When you interact with someone, the process is essentially two-way. Just as you will respond to the words and actions of another person, so he will do the same to you.

Over time from the day we are born, we all get to learn what is expected in our behavioural patterns to elicit the best responses from those with whom we are having a dialogue. At birth, a simple yowl is usually sufficient to get mum to come rushing forward to feed us, clean us and give us a cuddle. As we get older, however, we learn pretty rapidly that it is a question not just of getting the meaning of the words right, but also of the expressions that go with those words, the epithets that add politeness, respect, or whatever feelings we want to go with them, and the gestures that can also accompany such a dialogue.

The patterns of our personality are set very early on in childhood. Events and other people will have caused us to grow up the way we have, with all the self-doubts and prejudices that we have. The way in which our mothers and fathers treated us, for example, will have had a profound effect on our sense of worth. It is all too easy (and all too sad) for the most well-meaning adult to inflict all kinds of mental scars on his children. Being over-protective, for example, can lead a child to become over-reliant on others to fight his battles for him, leaving him with little sense of self-worth.

SIBLING RIVALRY WHEN HE WAS A KID

By holding back on displays of affection, an adult can lead a child into believing that he is unworthy of such love; by telling a child he is stupid, or that his brother or sister is 'better' than him, an adult can cause that child to do everything in so half-hearted a fashion that eventually it becomes a self-fulfilling prophecy.

Someone who has an unsettled childhood can also suffer in later life from being unable to form positive relationships with others. The effect of this is that he feels inadequate and inferior to his peers. And so we have a potential ever-decreasing spiral of self-image in the making.

These feelings of inadequacy translate into everyday behaviour and actions. We are all a product of our upbringing. When you next encounter the bullying type, instead of reacting with the inner thoughts 'What have I done to deserve this?', ask yourself what kind of an upbringing he might have had. Does he feel inadequate as a person, and are his bullying tactics perhaps a cover for the way he feels about himself?

Why are people difficult?

When we talk about dealing with difficult people, what we really mean is dealing with difficult behaviour. By learning to understand what it is that makes someone else behave and talk in a difficult way, we are in a better position not only to take charge of the situation, but also to help the other person resolve the conflicts that made him or her 'difficult' in the first place.

The crazy thing is that the natural way in which many of us react when we meet a difficult person is often more inclined to make that person's behaviour even more difficult. Ask yourself if you have ever reacted to someone by:

- sharply answering back
- becoming defensive rather than dealing with the problematical issue
- ignoring the meaning of what they are saying because you are so annoyed with the way they have spoken to you
- feeling confused and frightened
- becoming speechless with rage

The likelihood is that you will have experienced each of these reactions on numerous occasions. Many of us react in ways that make the problem worse; and yet, by stopping and thinking things through from the other person's perspective, by controlling the way we feel and attempting to act calmly and completely rationally, we can benefit in a number of ways:

- we will feel more in control
- by reducing our emotional reactions, we will be better able to think clearly and objectively
- we will feel less hampered by frustration or anger
- we will feel better about ourselves for not having responded like with like

So ask yourself – and be honest – do you let others dictate the way you feel about yourself? Turned round the other way, do you think your moods or actions could affect the behaviour and actions of another person?

WHAT YOU'RE SAYING MAKES PERFECT SENSE, LET'S TALK IT OVER

Let's face it, turning round a difficult person to become good-natured and easy to deal with is not something that you can achieve instantly. It may be that in time you can make him appreciate how unreasonable his behaviour is, and get him to change his ways. Over the short term, if you cannot change him, then maybe the next best thing is to change the way you react to him. After all, it is invariably the recipient of his behaviour who gets hurt or demoralised, rather than the difficult person himself.

Communication is a two-way process

All communication is a series of reactions and counter-reactions, if you think about it. Your difficult person will react to what you say in the same way as you will react to what he says. But if your reaction is different from what he is expecting, it is possible to break the cycle – to get him to counter-react in a different way from the way he was expecting to do – and very often this has the effect of defusing the unpleasant situation and improving communication between the two of you.

Everyone reacts to awkwardness in a different way. It's not surprising when you consider that some people might be shy and retiring whilst others are extrovert and over-confident. By making others feel low and bad about themselves, insecure people can give themselves a boost by inwardly telling themselves that they are better than others. By giving in to a bully, for instance, all you are doing is letting him win. But by responding in a calm and collected way, you can influence the way he counter-reacts to you, and often it is possible to do this without him even knowing.

We talked earlier on about the way in which you react to a difficult person. Do you normally answer back sharply to someone who needles you? Although perfectly natural, this response is hardly likely to improve the situation, except that in the short term you might feel better for being able to get your feelings off your chest. But what have you achieved? Difficult people are so used to behaving in a particular way, and leading their victims to react to them in such a way that they can then 'move in for the kill', that by denying them the wherewithal to play their trump card, you have effectively got the better of them. By not responding in a 'natural' way, you can break the cycle that your antagonist has set up for you to fall into. If you neither cower before a bullying manager, nor angrily explode at a subordinate, you effectively deny him the inner satisfaction of his own personal feel-good factor; and when difficult behaviour no longer works, most such antagonists fall back into a more reasonable frame of mind.

Suppose that one of your clients shouts at you for something that was clearly not your fault. (Many people manning telephone help desks get this kind of treatment on a regular basis.) You can respond in a number of ways. For instance, you could:

- defend both yourself and your company
- concentrate on his problem, rather than on your own feelings, recognising that the client is angry with the present situation – not at you. There is therefore no need to defend yourself.

The first response is likely to satisfy neither you nor your client. So why do it? You are simply allowing yourself to become the punch bag of your frustrated client. But if you concentrate on his problem, rather than your own feelings, as in the second alternative, the client is more likely to end up in a positive frame of mind and think better both of you and of your company.

Frankly, the customer is not interested in who made the mistake in the first place. All he wants is the problem to be resolved; and you will stay calmer if you don't become all defensive. In short, both sides win. So by taking a moment to reflect before you react, especially if you know that this person is difficult to deal with anyway, you have a much better chance of coming out on top. Simply having a shouting match brings you down to his level and achieves little.

Similarly, if one of your fellow workers shouts at you, for whatever reason, which of the following scenarios is most likely to be conducive to a healthy outcome?

- you fly into a rage and tell him what you think of him
- you pause and tell him in a calm and controlled manner that you feel angry about what he has just said

The first scenario is almost guaranteed to get him to scream back at you, and in the end neither of you will take the slightest notice of what the other is saying, regardless of whether there is any truth in what one or the other of you is saying. The second scenario, on the other hand, is far more assertive, and by controlling your emotions, you will also have much more likelihood of getting your point of view across.

If this person has a reputation for being difficult generally, it should also help that you know instinctively that it is not really you that is being attacked. Admittedly, it can still be pretty unpleasant being on the receiving end of such behaviour, but at least you can hold your head up knowing that if anyone is inadequate, it is he.

The classic example ...

How often have you been driving along a road when some inconsiderate motorist overtakes a whole stream of cars on a bend and all but causes an accident to happen in the process? It is, unfortunately, all too common an experience these days. The natural reaction of many is one of fury: to swear at the careless driver and to fume at all inconsiderate motorists. But in the process, their concentration lapses and their driving may suffer as a consequence. And the corollary of this is that other people then sound their horns because they are suffering from the bad driving of someone else. Meanwhile, the original driver who caused all the problems in the first place is miles away, probably upsetting yet more people at this very moment.

In this case, the ones to suffer are the 'victims' of that first bad driver. Anger would have been the perfectly natural reaction, but it has achieved nothing except to allow the actions of someone else to affect their feelings and judgement.

In the same way, if you allow yourself to become stressed at the behaviour of others, don't be surprised if the one to suffer most is you. Not only will you fail to get an adequate response from your protagonists, but you will, more than likely, be the one who is left feeling exhausted and emotionally drained.

Feeling inadequate

But getting angry with difficult people is not the only harmful way of reacting to them. It is just as bad if you don't stand up to them or if you make excuses and become all defensive. Think what you are saying to them with these kinds of responses. 'You're probably right and I'm really the one in the wrong.' Is that what you want to convey?

And what about feelings of negativity? Suppose you are due to go for an interview next Tuesday and you spend the previous week thinking of all the reasons why you may *not* get the job. Think about it: not only may your feelings of negativity cause you to see the worst in every situation, but it will also cause others to see the negative aspects in you. Rest assured, then, that if you go into the interview in this frame of mind, you will certainly not convey the best impression to the interviewer, thus confirming your worst fears to your inner self. And worse still, the entire week may have been ruined by your fear of the unknown.

Now think things through the opposite way round. Begin by making up a list of all the bad things that have happened to you this week. Study it well and ask yourself if any of these things would have happened without you there anyway. Now make a list of all the *good* things that have recently happened to you and of all the *good* characteristics that you can boast of. Doesn't it put it all into perspective?

We know of one married couple, who were going through a difficult patch, who every night wrote out a 'disaster diary' of everything that had gone wrong that day. It didn't matter how small or how annoying the 'disaster' was; everything got entered into that book. The wonderful thing was that when they read a given entry the following day or the next week or whenever, what had at the time appeared to be something dreadful became in time totally insignificant. The effect was that their marriage improved dramatically, and the feelings of negativity which had at one time appeared to hover over them like a black cloud, simply evaporated away.

So what do others think of you?

We have so far talked about the reactions we have to difficult people. But have you ever stopped to think about how others see *you*? It's all too easy to think that the way we see ourselves is the *same* as the way others see us. In fact, the opposite is much closer to the truth. Perhaps you believe it is important to say what you are thinking, regardless of the consequences. But how would you feel if someone treated you in the same way? In causing others distress by the things that you say, you are then no different from the difficult person that you suffered from before. How will others, then, regard you? The likelihood is that they will turn away from you, and you will end up feeling isolated. And it will be your fault entirely. Don't be surprised, then, if this leads you into more negativity in the way you treat others, and your behaviour gives others cause for concern.

What, then, can we do about it?
Despite our upbringing and effects that parents and other mentors have had on us, the fact is that the way we think of ourselves is not some immovable concept cast in stone. The great thing to realise is that we can actually choose to change our self-image.

We all have mini-disasters in our lives. Perhaps none are so public as those of professional sportspeople competing in international competitions. Even the best champion ice-skaters fall over; Premier Division footballers miss easy goals; and many a great cricketer has chided himself for being bowled out. But all of them realise that nothing is served by punishing oneself after the event. The ice-skater picks himself up and carries on; the footballer concentrates on lining up another goal; and as for the cricketer – well there is always another day!

It is only worth looking back at one's failures if there is a lesson to be learnt from them. And if you do learn from a mistake, then it can be regarded as something positive – not something to be ashamed of. So leave your failures behind you where they belong: in the past.

In the same way, you should try to build on your successes. Make a mental list of everything that you like about yourself. Even if you feel you are in the depths of depression, there is always something that you can find to add to that list if you think hard enough. People who have a poor image of themselves, for instance, often think that they can think of nothing good to say. The truth is, however, that such people are often highly sensitive and tend to be kind and compassionate. If those characteristics applied to a stranger that you met, you would react positively to them. So react positively about yourself and continue the list in that vein.

Now try listing the good things that have happened to you throughout your life. Everyone has successes, however small. Recall how good you felt when you had achieved those successes.

By learning to improve your self-image, you are more likely to be able to resist the damaging words and actions of difficult people; and by gaining a better insight into yourself you will automatically gain an insight into the way others act and speak; you may even begin to understand why they are acting the way they are; and once you can begin to feel pity for someone, however dreadful a person he is, you will find you no longer feel hurt by the things he says to you.

Later in this book you will learn the techniques of how to deal with all manner of difficult people in a variety of situations. By learning to deal with their moods and their own feelings of inadequacy, you will be more likely to succeed in coping with them and turn a potentially negative situation into one which will prove to be positive for both parties.

Summary

Today we have seen how the patterns of our personality are set very early on in childhood. In successfully dealing with difficult people, the key factor is to understand what makes them behave in the way they do. So the things we have to consider are:

- Perception of self-worth is often a main constituent of peoples' personalities
- Many of us react too quickly in ways that can make a problem worse
- Everyone reacts differently to awkward situations
- By becoming stressed in a difficult situation, you are likely to suffer more
- We can all choose to change our self-image and build on our successes

So, by learning to improve our self-image we are more likely to be able to resist the words and actions of difficult people.

Different styles of behaviour

When we talk about the different styles of behaviour of individuals, it is very easy to impart an almost limitless number of descriptions. For instance such people could be thought of as ogres, wimps, bullies, lecherous, uncaring, dominating, and so on. Yet, when you think of it, almost every behavioural style can be subsumed into one of three main categories:

> 1 Passive
> 2 Aggressive
> 3 Assertive

When dealing with difficult people it is important to be able to recognise the signs that they are exhibiting and to see these for what they are. That way, you can minimise the effects that they have on you, for it is a truism that you can really only expect to influence others when you can see them as they are, rather than as they would wish to be portrayed, or as you wish they were. Understanding someone's behaviour does not necessarily imply that you approve of it, but it does mean that you can cope with it, at worst, and work with it, at best.

Passive behaviour

Passive behaviour is most typified by people who put other people's needs before their own. Whilst on the one hand this can be an attractive trait in some, it can also show that they have little respect for themselves, especially when they are reluctant to stand up for their rights. The result is that they are often put upon by others, even by those who are not normally aggressive.

The passive person is usually pretty insecure and will often show signs of an inferiority complex. Just as he has little respect for his own abilities and will often talk down his gifts, his own feelings of inadequacy are reinforced every time he meets an aggressive type, and he is more likely to take criticism as justified without stopping to consider if that is in fact the case. He will often accept the criticism, and only at a later date will he question its validity. So, the passive person is often frustrated by his own inability to be assertive.

This hapless individual is also likely to be angry with himself since he can see how others take advantage of him; yet he is unlikely to do anything to improve the situation as he sincerely believes that others will not take him seriously. This in turn causes him to experience even greater feelings of inadequacy, and the whole situation becomes a vicious circle.

In summary, a passive person is likely to feel:

- angry, because he knows only too well that others are all too ready to take advantage of him and he finds it difficult not to let them
- anxious, because he feels he is not in control of his own destiny
- negative, because he feels that whatever he does, he is unlikely to get his way
- insecure, because he lacks self-confidence and is afraid of trying out anything new since he 'knows' instinctively that he will fail anyway
- frustrated, because he believes he cannot get his own way
- withdrawn, because no-one 'wants to listen to him'
- lacking in energy, because everything he does is to satisfy someone else's desires, rather than his own.

Until quite recently, it was considered normal for women to adopt a passive role – it was even expected. They 'knew their place', and cow-towed to their men-folk who held on to a traditional belief that their role was to be strong, to be the hunter, the breadwinner, the dominant partner in a marriage and to make the important decisions in any relationship. Strangely, it was also thought that men had more brain power and that women were emotionally unstable too. Only in recent years in Western societies has this attitude been shaken to its very foundations as sexual equality has started to follow in the wake of the Sixties' revolution, with women taking responsibility for both their bodies and their lifestyles, and they have learned to become more assertive in their behaviour.

Men, however, have had to start to unlearn their basic instincts in being the dominant species, especially in the workplace, and to exhibit more of the caring and feeling sides of their personalities.

The descriptions of passive behaviour above may appear at first reading to be extreme, and to an extent this is indeed the case; however, although the degree of passivity may vary, such people are all around us.

Now, wouldn't your first reaction in meeting such a person be one of sympathy for him and to want to help him boost his confidence? Well, unless you were a natural aggressor, you might well feel that. However, it is remarkable that after a very short time, the majority of those trying to help can end up feeling annoyed with the person for not trying to stand up for himself. This in turn can lead to an aggressive attitude towards that person because he has all but invited others to lose any kind of respect for him, and so they end up treating him the way he has come to expect to be treated!

When you try to compliment a passive person, he will often reject what you say. For instance, if you were to comment favourably on his tie, he might well respond that he has had it for ages, rather than accepting the compliment in the spirit in which it is given. It can, indeed, be quite tiring coping with someone who is so negative in everything he does and says, and it can also cause guilt feelings in oneself because you can feel responsible for that person being taken advantage of. Because of this, many will avoid passive, negative people, and this only acts to shore up their own feelings of inadequacy.

So just as passive people feel bad about themselves, others
dealing with passive people can feel:

- annoyed, because they wish they would just stand
  up for themselves occasionally
- worn out, because they feel they are wasting
  valuable energy dealing with their own negative
  reactions to such behaviour
- superior, because they have lost respect for
  someone who is unwilling to stand up for himself
- withdrawn, because such a negative attitude
  undermines their own positive attitude
- negative because of the amount of time needed to
  boost the passive person's ego before beginning to
  do the work or task in hand

Aggressive behaviour

Aggressive behaviour can best be summed up as satisfying
one's own needs at the expense of others. Such a person is
often a verbal bully who enjoys a feeling of power over
other people. But just as physical bullying is often the
outward manifestation of someone who is cowardly by
nature, oddly enough, aggressive behaviour is often the
result of feelings of inadequacy and lack of self-worth. In
that respect, aggressive behaviour is the classic bedfellow
of the passive-behaviour person.

Aggressive people are also, as often as not, lonely. Their
behaviour results in others shunning them, both in their
personal lives and at work. They are so busy reassuring
themselves that they are the best, that they end up being

overly critical of others. Nothing is ever *their* fault, and by extension, anything that goes wrong is due to someone else. Their lack of self-esteem does not allow them to admit faults.

People who exhibit aggressive tendencies often feel:

- energetic, except that their energy is often destructive rather than constructive
- powerful, because they enjoy having others rush around carrying out their orders
- somewhat guilty, since they know they take advantage of others
- lonely, because their aggression alienates them from other people
- that they are always right, and that they have a monopoly of good ideas
- threatened, in case others might see through the veneer of outward confidence
- exasperated by the passive people who don't share their energy and speed

Some people are inclined to mistake aggression for strength and act accordingly, in the belief that if they show others a 'soft underbelly', they will be regarded as weak. But such behaviour is more inclined to have the reverse effect on others, who may feel angry or frustrated because they might be powerless to do anything about it. For instance, if a manager behaves in such a way to a subordinate, the latter may be fearful of losing his job if he tells his boss exactly what he thinks of him. The 'victim' will therefore be resentful of the way in which he has been treated, but the aggressor may not even realise that he has caused such feelings in the subordinate. The end result is one of a breakdown in communication, with a resulting lack of efficiency and with neither party understanding where 'things have gone wrong'. In these cases it can be a very uphill job to rescue the situation once the patterns of behaviour have been established.

So, people who exhibit aggressive behaviour can cause *others* to feel:

- defensive, because they feel that anything they do will be attacked unfairly
- resentful, because the aggressor appears to wield power unfairly
- threatened, because they resent such tactics
- humiliated, because no-one likes to be made a fool of
- frustrated, because they are always having to be on the defensive
- withdrawn, because they try to avoid possible confrontations with the aggressor

Those who deal regularly with an aggressive person are inclined to suffer high levels of stress, and this can have a damaging effect on their well-being. The aggressor, on the other hand, enjoys his apparent feelings of power since it appears to boost his authority. The result is that people tend to avoid aggressors if they possibly can, which in turn leads the latter to believe they are somehow special. And this makes them act even more aggressively, and once again we have a vicious circle.

Assertive behaviour

The third category of person that we mentioned at the start of this chapter is the *assertive person*. He it is who is concerned not only for his own rights and opinions, but also for the rights and opinions of others. In trying to obtain a win–win situation with others, the assertive person is willing to make compromises in a positive way, at the same time arguing his corner for what he passionately believes in.

Because respect plays an important part in the assertive person's attitude, it engenders respect in the attitudes of others with whom he is in daily contact, encouraging them to co-operate as fully as possible with that person. This in itself produces a healthy atmosphere in which creative work can be carried out and in which people know their work will be appreciated by others. All in all, this then leads those others to do their level best to perform even better, whatever the job in hand.

An assertive person is also one who is able to understand his own feelings and can impart how he feels to others. The trick is to be able to explain what you feel in such a way that you will not cause others to resent what you say. The reality is that people are much more comfortable knowing where they stand, even if there is implied criticism of their position, rather than having to guess at the real meaning behind the words.

Being assertive means you can be proud of your successes; but equally it means that you are not conceited about your achievements. It also means that you can learn from your mistakes, that no-one has a monopoly on good ideas and that others can catch the enthusiasm that is such a characteristic of the assertive person.

People who can best be described as assertive often exhibit the following tendencies:

- They approach new tasks in a positive frame of mind
- They are enthusiastic in their approach
- They are honest in dealing with others
- They are energetic, and direct that energy into reaching their goals
- They have good communication skills with others
- They are willing to take risks, but at the same time they know their own limitations
- They understand that other people have needs and feelings just as they do

Assertive people are generally the ones other people most like to be associated with. Because they are not seen as manipulative, people work easily with them. Because their behaviour is consistent, communication is open and trusted.

Regular communication lets others know what is expected of them, and so the whole team is able to turn its energies to achieving goals, rather than infighting and self-recrimination.

When dealing with assertive people, others are most likely to feel positive because:

- they sense that their success is a shared success
- they know where they stand
- they can reciprocate feelings of respect
- they can direct their energies into constructive areas
- they feel they can trust you and respond to your positive influence by helping you
- they will find the enthusiasm contagious

Now, from the above, it must be perfectly clear that the most desirable camp to be in is the assertive group. Most of us, however, exhibit a mixture of different styles, and so to succeed in minimising the negative effects of difficult behavioural patterns in others, it is necessary to move oneself as far as possible into the assertive area.

Who wins, after all?

Passive people rarely achieve their own goals because they seldom identify their own goals in the first place, relying on others to give them a lead.

Aggressive people often achieve their goals in the short term, but often this is at the expense of others and this fact can then backfire on them at a later date when they come face to face with antagonism and retaliation from those whom they have put down in the past. Worse still, there is no loyalty engendered in others during the process of 'winning', and so there is no pool of loyalty on which they can draw when times get tough.

It is assertive people who usually achieve their goals because in their view everyone can win. They are willing to negotiate for what is right rather than for short-term expediency, and they gain the respect of others whilst doing so. Enlightened self-awareness can enable us to get into the right attitude to make the most of our own assertiveness, but we will deal with this later.

On Wednesday and Thursday we will see how putting ourselves into the balanced assertiveness camp can help us in handling conflict as well as with our basic communication skills.

Summary

Most styles of behaviour can be categorised in three basic ways:

1 Passive
2 Aggressive
3 Assertive

and in order to be able to deal with difficult people successfully, you need to recognise them for what they are.

- What would you say are the main characteristics of each?
- Which would you rather be yourself?
- Can you identify the most difficult person in your life at the moment? In what style of behaviour would you categorise him?

Coping with different problem people

What do we mean by problem people? They come in all shapes and sizes, but the one common trait that they all exhibit is a type of behaviour that gives someone else a problem.

If you put your mind to it, you would probably be able to come up with at least 50 different types of behaviour that can cause problems for others. Being able to distinguish and categorise a particular type of behaviour will put you in a much better position to be able to do something about it. Of course, you could always ignore the problem, but that isn't very constructive and could even make the problem worse for others as well as for yourself. If you cannot even recognise what it is that someone does or says that causes problems for others, how on earth are you going to be able to improve that person's behaviour for the future – or, more to the point, your reaction to it?

Not all people problems are necessarily daunting. Some types of behaviour might be a trifle irritating, but are easy enough to shrug off without anything further needing to be done. Others, on the other hand, seem to have a never-ending impact and they can leave you feeling totally at a loss to work out how best to cope.

Very often, the person whose behaviour causes problems is totally unaware of the conflict he causes for others. That being the case, it works out that the person who has to deal with the problem is actually you. You have to 'own' the problem, just as if you were 'owning' a problem of late delivery or total quality production in a factory.

Yet, however inconsiderate or boorish someone else's behaviour, it is equally true that we all react to one another, and the way someone else reacts to you has a feedback effect on the way you behave in the first place. Sometimes we are therefore actually responsible for the problematic behaviour in others. Whilst one could regard this as part and parcel of life's rich tapestry, it does matter, not least because:

- it creates unnecessary stress, leading to low morale
- it wastes time, because effort is being expended on griping instead of on productive work and relationships
- it distorts the decision-making process, since those who display difficult behaviour are often circumvented in order to ease the burden on others
- it can encourage a selective emigration of the best employees to more conducive working environments
- it stops work being in any way fun

When encountering a difficult person for the first time, it is all too easy to hate him or to label him as deficient in some way without properly understanding what it is that he himself is going through. Yet if you are serious about wanting to change his behaviour, you will only be able to do so if you learn to understand him from his own point of view. Pigeonholing people on sight is one of the most destructive things you can do within a workplace or community.

Within a work environment, it might appear that those with behavioural problems can be broken down into three main categories:

1 your supervisors
2 your subordinates
3 your fellow co-workers

The supervisors might be poor motivators, aggressive, or have poor supervisory skills; the subordinates might be error-prone, daydreamers, time wasters, or dishonest; whilst the co-workers might exhibit unprofessional behaviour such as putting things off, 'passing the buck', being overly critical or shirking.

Whilst the way in which you might deal with the person will vary, depending on where they are in the hierarchical structure relative to you, each of these categories of worker can display common behavioural problems. So let's look at some of the more common types of behaviour and consider how we might deal with them.

Although there are very many types of personality display, we have chosen to break down the different behavioural patterns into four main categories:

1 *insecure* – one of the most basic reasons for people displaying problematic behaviour;
2 *negative* – it can be very wearing to deal with this when exposed to such behaviour for long periods;
3 *selfish* – whether they are consciously so or oblivious to the fact that they are what they are, these types are easier to diagnose and to 'turn around';

4 *pleasant* – this is sometimes the most difficult type
of behaviour to deal with as you do not want to hurt
their feelings.

Insecure people

Insecurity in people can take a number of forms. In its most
basic, the insecure person needs to boost his own self-
image, but the problem is that he does this by criticising
others. The eternal put-down can be very wearing, and if
this then turns into your being hurt or even becoming
openly hostile in return, it can have a bad effect on any
kind of working relationship.

Perhaps worse still is the type who is, on the surface,
perfectly pleasant to begin with, until something that most
would regard as quite innocuous causes him to lose control
and let fly with insults. Basically, this type of person has
never quite got over the habit of his childhood tantrums
and is turning on a defence mechanism; perhaps he feels
personally threatened, or under pressure. His immediate
reaction, therefore, is to react before anyone has even
launched an attack on him.

Insecurity also makes itself felt by the ponderous types
who either cannot make up their minds, or will always find
some reason for putting off any kind of action. It may be
that this kind of person has such low self-esteem that he is
afraid that anything he does will be wrong, even though he
genuinely wants to help. Equally, however, it may be that
he simply does not feel that anyone else's efforts are good
enough, and having asked someone to do something for

him, he will then set about doing exactly the same task himself just to 'make sure' that the information, or whatever, is adequate.

On a bad day, dealing with insecure people can leave you wondering whether the effort is worthwhile. Yet all such responses need to attempt to build up that person's self-esteem by not knocking him down when he is – perhaps subconsciously – expecting that very reaction. Reassurance is all, but in addition you should attempt:

- never to snap back, since this is what he may expect, and so by refraining from doing so you are breaking a vicious circle
- to be assertive in attempting to find out what the problem is from his point of view and to understand what is troubling him
- to remain absolutely silent if he is throwing a temper tantrum, and only then to ask him to explain himself
- to set deadlines for those normally incapable of setting timescales for themselves. This gives them confidence that it is not just they who are having to take responsibility for meeting deadlines.

You can also use humour to get you through difficult times with problem people. Some even recommend conjuring up a mental image of the difficult person to relieve the stress of having to be on the receiving end of some of his tirades. For instance, if your boss throws a temper tantrum, try picturing him still wearing a nappy and throwing his toy out of his pram. Such an image can do wonders to keep oneself calm whilst others around are losing their cool.

Negative people

Negativity in a person is also very tiring to deal with and can be extremely depressing because if one is not careful it can almost infect you – in the same way that one person yawning in a room can often 'infect' others with the same action.

Such people may well be trying to protect themselves from future failure, but in so doing their immediate reaction is to ask 'What's the point ... ?' Rarely will they come up with any better suggestions for carrying out a task. Worse, if you attempt to offer an alternative solution you are likely to get a similar negative response.

Another type of negative person is the aggressive, verbal bully – the type who believes he knows better than anyone else how something should be done and doesn't waste a moment in telling everyone of his infallibility. He will often tell you that you are wasting your time because you are not doing things his way. As often as not he is very thorough and highly efficient, but that does not stop others from feeling resentment and ignoring him on principle.

The first thing when dealing with such people is not to let their negativity invade you. In addition you could:

- try to get him to explain why he feels as he does
- tell him that as you are convinced in your own mind as to the right course of action, you will do so anyway, regardless of whether he is 'with' you or not
- resist wasting time arguing with him
- make sure you have done your homework before tackling the negative, assertive bully
- ask yourself whether at the end of the day it is worth dealing with such a person anyway since he is unlikely to change his behaviour and will continue to give you grief for some time to come!

Selfish people

Selfish people often act the way they do without pausing to consider for one moment that what they are doing is destructive or hurtful to others. Sometimes they are as they are because in childhood their parents had never trained them out of their natural selfish state that we are all born with. (Consider a baby crying, for instance. As far as he is concerned, his comforts are all that matters, and naturally, he has not yet learned that others have needs too.)

Very often, selfish people can be extremely irritating. If your next-door neighbour in a block of flats has his stereo system turned up too loud, he may well turn it down when asked to, but if he is basically selfish he will, as sure as anything, forget the next time around and have it up at full blast once again.

Selfish people will often be so busy telling others of their thoughts and needs, that they may be oblivious to the fact that others might have something to say, or an opinion to share. Those who bulldoze their way through life can be extremely disruptive in a work environment. Since they are so busy trying to get their own way, their co-workers may put up with this for a while, but soon they start to build up resentment which leads them to ostracise that person, or worse still, they may lose their temper with them. However, that is the last thing one should do since the selfish person will invariably win this type of 'argument'.

Another type of selfish behaviour is displayed by a fundamentally aggressive person who is covert in his attacks on others. The end result of this person's making jokes at others' expense, normally behind their backs, can be that the victim is much more hurt than he would be if the 'joke' had been made out in the open. If the victim then takes offence, the aggravator can accuse the victim of being a bad sport, or of not being able to 'take a joke'.

This type of person thrives in front of an audience but will rarely continue such behaviour in private. So, to attempt to change his behaviour, you should:

- get him on his own, explain what he is doing and ask if he is genuinely trying to hurt you
- avoid getting into an argument with him, but do stand up to him and keep your body language assertive
- not sound either angry or submissive as this will feed his feelings of superiority
- if he is making derogatory remarks about you behind your back, suggest that in future he make them directly to you. He won't!

Pleasant people

Perhaps the most difficult people to deal with are those who are on the surface pleasant in their ways. This is because it makes us feel guilty to confront them with their problematic behaviour, especially if they react in a manner that shows that they are hurt that anyone could have found something wrong with them.

Not all pleasant, problematic people are wimps, of course. Whilst some might keep a low profile because they are genuinely confused, others may be perfectly nice but just unreliable. Yet again, someone might be anxious to gain respect and friendship, but be unwilling to make any efforts to achieve this.

Some unreliable people need so much to feel liked by everyone, that they will promise to do all kinds of things, and only subsequently realise that they cannot deliver their promises. They then feel obliged to make even more promises to make up for their earlier shortcomings, and a vicious circle sets in.

Although it can be embarrassing to deal with such people, they are probably the most worthwhile in the end to have to deal with since there is a good chance that you can turn them around to face the realities of a situation and they can then become valued players in a team. The trick here is to offer reassurance that they are likeable and that their views are valued, just so long as they are willing to say what they think, rather than agree with everyone simply to make the peace.

In addition, you should:

- keep your body language open and friendly
- reassure them that you value their opinions
- pay them compliments, so long as these are genuine, in order to demonstrate that they really are valued members of the team
- encourage them to come up with suggestions and solutions to problems
- help them save face by stating the facts, rather than your opinions, and then getting them to suggest ideas of their own

NO NO, YOUR WORK RECORD IS EXCELLENT, IT'S JUST THAT ...

We said at the beginning of this chapter that it should be easy enough to think of at least 50 different types of problematic behaviour. The four main categories that we have just looked at will not necessarily encompass every one, just as many problem people will exhibit characteristics of more than one of them. But by reaching out and attempting to understand what it is that drives someone to behave in the way that he does, you will have a better chance of being able to turn him around from being a difficult person to a valued member of your team.

Summary

We have spent Tuesday looking at behavioural problems exhibited by difficult people. If you really want to change their behaviour, the best way forward is to try to see how the world looks through their eyes.

- Is your difficult person insecure, negative, selfish or pleasant?
- How do you think you should approach dealing with him now?
- How do you think you should modify your behaviour when dealing with him?
- Is this achievable?

Managing conflict situations

Unfortunately, there is nothing unusual about conflict. It is an integral part of life, and without the differences between us we would all be the poorer. Just imagine how boring things would become if we all thought and reacted in the same way!

But just as, paradoxically, we need conflict to brighten up our lives, we also need to be able to manage it so that it does not get out of hand and start to dominate a situation, for in that case it can lead to highly stressful times.

Conflicts invariably stem from one root cause: in essence both sides want to have their own way, and unless a compromise is achieved, conflict is inevitable. Throughout our lives, we have to come to terms with the conflicting forces of logic and emotion. Sometimes it is all too easy to react emotionally, but inevitably it is when our reactions are based on logic that we are better able to handle difficult circumstances. We must also not forget that the emotional content of our relationships gives them their raison d'être and comfort zones – as well as the potential for conflict. Emotion must be valued too.

To many people, it is much more difficult to get into gear with a logical approach, but it is, nonetheless, perfectly possible to develop the ability to use logic by first analysing the situation and then applying techniques to control your feelings and reactions instead of allowing your emotions to rule the day.

It is really down to a question of:

- Let's step back and look at the situation a bit more clearly
- Let's get the emotion out of this
- How can we move this situation forward toward achieving the common objectives?

Only then can individual problems and sensitivities be accommodated rather than their dominating and waylaying progress within the relationships.

There are, of course, many reasons for conflict between two parties. For instance:

- each may wish to achieve different goals
- there is a difference in the perception of the problems involved
- there is a clash of personality which stifles communication
- each party may be in competition with one another
- either party might not want the responsibility imposed by a certain course of action
- there is poor communication

Although such conflict can cause depression or apathy, it is equally true that many stressful situations can lead to positive results, such as the generation of enthusiasm or the finding of a solution to a problem that had remained stubbornly impenetrable. So the problem is not actually a situation where there is conflict, but more one where the conflict is negative – where stress turns itself into distress.

The real danger of stressful conflict is that it can be so damaging. For instance:

- it can divert attention away from the real issues behind the conflict, and the objectives can be lost
- one or both parties to the conflict can become so frustrated that it impedes a settlement, and ultimately one or both sides become unco-operative

Many conflict situations arise because one of the parties feels that someone is attempting to take advantage of him, or because he feels he has to defend himself against an aggressive person. Basically, when any conflict situation arises there are three possible outcomes:

1 both sides can pretend there is really no problem. If the matter is not particularly important, then this can often be the best outcome;
2 one person wins, whilst the other loses. This may solve the present conflict, but it can lead to a build-up of resentment and make it more difficult to resolve the next crisis point;
3 each person understands that the final solution has to take account of both parties' wishes. By working to a common goal, both sides have to make compromises, but the final solution is stronger because of this.

In understanding what situations lead to conflict, a person will more easily be able to avoid it. There are, of course, no hard and fast rules about reducing potential conflicts, but the following list demonstrates some of the areas which are ripe for examination:

- By attempting to see things from other people's points of view, you are better able to accept that no one person is ever always right or wrong
- It is equally not possible for everyone always to agree on everything. By accepting the fact that compromise is better than conflict, you are better able to find a way forward, rather than wallowing in an impasse
- Many of us are all too prone to make snap judgements. It follows from the above that if we can hear out the other person without jumping to conclusions, we will be better able to find a way forward

When it comes to recognising the early stages of a conflict in the making, very often the cause has more to do with the characters involved, rather than the situation itself. For, if logic is the most positive way of resolving a conflict, then it follows that wherever emotion gets a stranglehold, then a resolution can become more difficult.

When it comes to determining different personality types with regard to handling conflict, most people can be diagnosed as being in one of four basic categories: *dictatorial, enthusiastic, empathetic* and a *processor*.

Dictators

Perhaps the most difficult type of personality to come to terms with, dictatorial people tend to be egoists in the extreme. They always want to have their own way and will often bulldoze people into submission. Often they can be extremely hurtful because they say what they think regardless of how others will react. They are totally results-oriented and have little time for individuals.

The problem in dealing with such people is that being aggressive in return is generally counter-productive. Similarly, acting submissively will only reinforce their feelings of superiority. The only sure way of interacting with a dictator is to deal in facts, for to them, facts are an extension of logic. This will also enable you to get to the heart of the matter at the earliest opportunity, and to reach a solution. They may well have alienated you in the process, but ultimately that will be their problem. The main thing to ensure is that it should not be yours!

Enthusiastic people

Enthusiasts are normally energetic and have a strong ability to motivate others. They can often be described as charismatic and are often popular. Enthusiasts are sometimes wont to talk rapidly and loudly, but ultimately if they do not get the necessary feedback they are more likely to drop out of a project before seeing it through to completion.

Dealing with enthusiasts requires you to be almost as energetic as they are. Offering support and encouragement are the most likely ways to get the best out of them and to work with them – and to get any project happily completed.

Empathisers

Into this camp fall what are sometimes referred to as 'people persons'. They are typically genuinely caring but are not the best at getting things done in a hurry, and can be frustratingly indecisive.

Accordingly, if you want to get the best from an empathiser it is wise not to hurry him, and to listen attentively to what he has to say.

Processors

Such people, who may appear somewhat tedious or boring on the outside, nevertheless exhibit analytical skills that involve paying great attention to detail. They are usually efficient, if a little on the unimaginative side, and organised in the extreme. Processor types often end up in professions such as accountancy where accuracy and detail are paramount; but it is not for nothing that comedians tend to use them for the butt of their jokes (e.g.: Monty Python's 'Ich bin ein Chartered Accountant' sketch).

Dealing with processor types invariably works well when presenting them with logic and facts. They are not always the fastest thinkers as they like to assimilate new information, building on, and assessing it with, what they already know.

As we have said, not everyone falls precisely into one category or another. But it soon becomes clear, when taking these four basic types, that conflict can easily arise if, for instance, a processor comes into discussion with a dictatorial person, or an enthusiast has to deal with an empathiser.

Just as it can be quite exasperating to deal with colleagues at work, it is often even more problematic dealing with difficult clients or customers. The old axiom that 'the client is always right' may well form the backbone of customer service, but it can leave employees feeling frustrated and stressed.

Those at the receiving end of a customer's anger – be they at the end of a phone, or in a meeting face to face – are often the main point of contact between a client and a company, and so they become the butt of the client's anger. Yet, reacting in an impatient or insensitive manner is not the way to get the customer to move over to your point of view, and certainly not the stuff of professional customer service.

Nowadays, especially, where customer service is what differentiates one company from another in an increasingly global marketplace, any form of negative behaviour or reaction from a company employee could result in a customer staying away and taking his business elsewhere. Worse still, he may tell his friends and they could stay away too. Trying to win a customer back is twice as difficult as landing him in the first place – as if that wasn't hard enough! So, the way in which an employee acts with, and reacts to, a customer can be far more important than the advertising or PR that a company puts together to build up its image.

Successfully dealing with difficult clients necessitates putting yourself in the client's shoes and understanding what it is that makes him annoyed, or even more basically, what he wanted in the first place. There are at least two sides from which to look at every situation, and people don't generally complain unless they have something specific to 'beef' about.

In general, a customer can get annoyed with a company for one of five main reasons:

1 he feels no-one will listen to him;
2 something went wrong, and he feels no-one is willing to accept responsibility;
3 he needs help or guidance, but can find no-one to give it to him;
4 the product does not work, or the service provided is inadequate;
5 he thought through and planned everything to do with the purchase or installation, and yet it still went wrong.

By finding out what it is that the client is unhappy about, you can then concentrate on solving his problem.

Remember, he is not necessarily interested in a third party finding a solution. As far as he is concerned, you are the company representative and so it is up to you to find a solution. Your blaming another part of the organisation will only inflame the situation further.

It may not, of course, be possible for you to be the solution provider. So what should you do? The first thing is to attempt to find a position of empathy with his plight. Nothing is more frustrating than feeling that no-one understands your problem. So, by showing understanding and getting over to his side, you are immediately getting rid of his first frustration. Only then should you start to help deal with the problem.

Sometimes, customers are not really sure what they do want, apart from tearing someone off a strip for the wrongs they feel they have suffered. So a good technique is, having empathised with their situation, to ask what they would like you to do to help out. It may well be that you personally can't help him in this case; so state what you can do, offering one or two alternatives. You have effectively returned control of the situation to the customer. Sometimes there will be nothing at all that you can do – in which case you will need to explain the company's policies and try to find with him a common solution. By spending time showing sympathy and understanding, you might not have put things totally to rights, but your client will know that he is not likely to get the brush-off – which is what angers people the most.

Dealing with someone face to face is often easier than doing so over the telephone because you can use body language to convey your feelings. However, there are some standard dos and don'ts when dealing with difficult clients over the phone:

- You should always follow the '3 Ps' code: come across as professional, polite and pleasant
- The caller must be made to feel important
- You should try to avoid wasting not just the caller's time, but the company's time as well
- You want to help the caller achieve his desired objectives

Whether the conflict situation is over the phone or face to face, you should always remain cool and calm and do your best to appear concerned but impartial at all times. There is nothing wrong with expressing contradictory ideas, but the secret is in knowing how to put them across without it escalating into a heated debate.

At the end of the day, it is not the fact that you have a contradictory idea that causes problems; more, it is the fact that two personality traits come into opposition. The first should not be smothered; the latter should be circumvented if at all possible.

Summary

On Wednesday we looked at the likely causes of conflict and why they can lead to such damaging and stressful situations. When you look logically at the people involved, bearing in mind the emotional content:

- can you identify the goals that each has?
- does each see the problem the same way?
- is there a problem of 'personal chemistry'?
- are they all working to the same objectives?
- are any of them reluctant to stand up and be counted?
- are there any communications problems?
- what are the *real* issues anyway?

If you have a situation of real conflict now, or can see one arising, can you identify which personality type best describes the difficult person with whom you have to deal?

Basic communications skills and body language

Communication is at the heart of any relationship between two people; and very often a lack of good communication is the single most important barrier to getting on with a so-called 'difficult person'.

Anyone who feels he is consistently misunderstood is often guilty of nothing more than his own propensity to make assumptions. What you think you say and what someone else understands you to say are very often not the same. For instance, you might *think* you say something, but *actually* say something else. Someone else might *think* you said something but *actually* hear something else. He might then *think* he has responded to you in a certain way, but *actually* respond differently, and you might *think* he has responded in a certain way even though you *actually* heard him say something else. Confused? So you should be. It was all wrapped up rather nicely when Humpty Dumpty said, 'Words mean what you want them to mean.'

Luckily, good communication is not just about speaking and listening. Although they are obviously very important, the words only account for a small proportion of any useful amount of comprehension between two people. The intonation and expressions inherent in the voice are also key factors, as are the messages contained in what we call 'body language'.

Even though a speaker may actually be perfectly coherent, he may still be misunderstood. This is often as much to do with the listener as the speaker. Consider, for instance, if the listener:

- has a low level of concentration – he may not actually be taking in what you are saying
- is prejudiced in some way – in which case he will automatically be colouring the meaning of what you are saying
- has a headache – he is more likely to be distracted from listening attentively
- has no background experience of what you are saying – in which case, how will he assimilate new material when there is no 'peg' in his mind on which to hang it?
- is stressed in some way – he is unlikely to be able to concentrate
- feels that he is out of his depth in the subject matter and therefore *expects* not to understand

There are numerous other reasons why someone might not take on board all your instructions. Often the use of paraphrasing what you are saying is a good way around this problem as what it does is to reach the listener from a number of different viewpoints, thereby offering a better chance for the message to get through. It also shows that the message is getting through in the way that the speaker intended. In this way misunderstandings can be avoided – and that has to be a good thing in any communication situation.

Feedback is another important part of the communication process. This can not only show how you react to something someone is saying, but can also help the speaker clarify his message if this is not getting through.

To amplify, it is entirely appropriate to offer feedback in order to let others know when:

- you have understood what they are saying
- you have *not* understood what they are saying
- you are upset or embarrassed about what they have said
- you disagree with what they are saying
- you approve of what they are saying
- you are amused by what they have said

Gossip plays an essential part in communication processes. It can reinforce the interest, understanding and comfort in one another and thereby it can put you on a common plain when communicating one with another. A little social intercourse can often identify potential problems before they turn into a conflict.

In giving feedback, you should:

- make sure that the speaker is ready to receive your contra-messages
- be specific, rather than give 'woolly' examples
- do so as soon as possible after the event so that the subject is still 'warm' in the speaker's mind
- do so in private if at all possible, if it is a sensitive situation, since it can be quite damaging if done in front of others
- be positive in order to lead the situation forward
- encourage the recipient to give feedback in a like manner in order that no-one is seen to be scoring points at the other's expense

Of course, some people are much more difficult to deal with than others, and there is always a danger, when giving feedback to a difficult person, that your attempt could backfire, especially if he is higher up than you in the management hierarchy. In such cases, advance preparation is absolutely essential:

- You must begin by identifying the problem and concentrating on what can be improved by the person in question
- If possible, you should try to determine why the person is behaving in such a manner
- You should always be prepared for a confrontation if giving a difficult person feedback about his general or specific behaviour. How will you handle his reactions? Try to imagine what defence he will come up with
- Rehearse both your arguments and counter-reactions thoroughly so that you know instinctively what you are going to do or say at the right time
- Be positive in what you are saying to the difficult person. Explain simply why what he does or says upsets you, and express your willingness to help him to adapt his ways
- Try to work out and agree a plan of action on both his and your part
- Comment positively on progress that you observe in his behaviour in order to encourage him further

We mentioned earlier on that speech and listening are only two parts of any communication process. But being able to interpret non-verbal signals is also an extremely important adjunct in ensuring understanding.

All of us have a propensity to 'hear' other people by observing their physical reactions. Indeed, it is said that you can sometimes tell much more from watching someone than from listening to what they are saying. Usually this feedback is positive in that it reinforces what someone is saying, at the same time demonstrating what we feel inside. But equally, body language can give false signals which can override the verbal message that is being given out, and thereby harm the communication process.

There are very many types of body language, just a few of which are shown below. What do you read into the situation when you see someone:

- frowning? Usually this indicates that he either disagrees with what is being said or simply doesn't understand
- avoiding eye contact? This is a sure sign that he is bored or lacks confidence, or perhaps he has something to hide
- scratching his nose? He may be puzzled or may dislike something, but equally he may just have an itchy nose!
- speaking rapidly? Perhaps he is anxious or worried
- raising his voice? It is likely that he is angry or worried
- shifting from one foot to the other? He might be impatient, but equally he might have been standing for too long!

People who lie often give themselves away by their body language, whilst those who are genuine are usually easy to spot. Liars will often avoid looking directly at you whilst blinking or swallowing rapidly, clearing the throat or covering their mouths whilst speaking.

It is not for nothing that the expression 'having a poker face' is used to convey the picture of someone who has so mastered the control over his involuntary body movements that it is well nigh impossible to guess what he is thinking. But would you trust someone with a poker face? Whatever it was that he said, the chances are that you would instinctively mistrust him.

Variations in the amount of eye contact can also tell you a great deal about the person with whom you are conversing. Think back to when you were last angry with someone. Did you look him right in the eye as you spoke to him? As a rule of thumb, most people are comfortable with eye contact for up to around five seconds. Anything more than that and it can make the recipient feel uncomfortable – which is exactly why aggressive people stare out those whom they feel to be their inferiors.

Fixing someone with a stare is not the same action, of course, that people in love appear to enjoy. If you look at the latter, their eyes dart backwards and forwards between the eyes and across the face – very different from a single fixed stare.

When people blink a lot, this can also be a sign that they are nervous, which itself may be an indication that they are not being entirely truthful with you – but they might also be contact-lens wearers and therefore need to blink a lot!

On the other hand, if someone hardly blinks at all, this could be an indication that they are either listening intently to what you are saying or watching for your reactions. As always, there is no hard and fast rule about what to look out for, but rather it is a combination of different signs.

So, summing up, what should we look out for when trying to sum up someone's body language? Getting back to our three types of behaviour – aggressive, passive and assertive – there are certain behavioural patterns that become all too obvious.

For instance, someone who is assertive will usually maintain good eye contact, be relaxed and will smile or nod to encourage the other person as he speaks. A submissive person, on the other hand, will often lower his eyes in a downcast position so as to avoid eye contact; he might have a poor posture such as slouching or drooping his shoulders, and he might cover his mouth with his hand in a defensive posture. Someone who is aggressive, however, will often maintain unwavering eye contact whilst standing with his feet apart and placing his hands on his hips in an impatient manner.

These same three behavioural types can also be identified from such a simple thing as shaking hands. For instance, an aggressor will often tend to grasp your hand with his own uppermost and his palm facing downwards. A passive person will offer his palm face up, whilst the assertive type tends to shake your hand at the same angle as yours – i.e. at right angles to the floor.

But you can take it even further than this. How often have you been to a party and experienced all manner of handshakes? There's the traditional limp shake whereby a floppy hand suggests that here is a weak and indecisive person. On the other hand, someone who grasps your hand tightly may well be the type of person who wants to show he is both tough and in complete control. People who proffer just their fingers and thumb rather than their whole hand are as often as not insecure, whilst someone who holds his arm out stiffly might covertly be suggesting to you that he intends to be in control of the entire situation. However, you still have to bear in mind any physical disabilities in this too. The person who does not notice rheumatoid arthritis in a hand that he has to shake may cause anxiety and pain when shaking hands firmly instead of the friendly gesture that was intended.

Non-verbal language can therefore be very useful in summing up a particular type of person. Body language often reflects a person's mental approach to life, and difficult people, in particular, will often give themselves away by their actions – both voluntary and involuntary. By learning to read the signs, you will be in a much better position to adjust your own responses and to be in better control of the situation.

Summary

Today we have been examining the necessity for offering feedback in a two-way communication process and the need to think through different ways of offering feedback that will be positive to the situation. These are:

- paraphrasing
- clearly stating specific examples of the point in question
- being sensitive to the feelings of others
- body language – in all its forms

How to say 'no' and deal with difficult clients

Most people find it difficult to say 'no'. It is in our nature not to do so for a number of reasons, not least because we all feel the need to be liked and to be appreciated, and refusing a request can make us appear selfish to others.

The problem is that by not being able to say what we really feel on such occasions, there is not just a possibility, but a distinct likelihood that we will become over-burdened, and this can lead to stress and worry. This is particularly true in the workplace where by agreeing to do everything that is asked of you, you could end up with an in-tray a mile high, whilst others appear to cope much more easily.

Nobody likes to feel he is being taken advantage of, yet a person who has difficulty saying 'no' is the very type to feel put upon by his work colleagues. If he refuses to do what is asked of him, he may well feel that he will no longer be liked or appreciated by the person doing the asking. He might even be fearful of an aggressive reaction if he says 'no' and therefore caves in since he may feel it is the better of the two options to cope with.

The point is, though, that by failing to make a stand you are more likely to store up problems for the future. For instance, if you were really too busy to take on some extra work, no-one will thank you for handing in something that has been rushed and is of low quality. By avoiding causing displeasure in the first place by not refusing to take something on, you are much more likely to compound the problem at a later date.

Such a scenario is especially true where a boss hands a subordinate vast amounts of work, knowing that that person is normally efficient and trustworthy. In reality, the subordinate might be unwilling to say 'no' because:

- he does not wish to appear inefficient or incapable of completing the task
- he is afraid that his boss will get angry and that ultimately this could put his job 'on the line'
- he wants to be liked and appreciated by all his work colleagues
- he has low self-esteem and wants to build up the esteem of others

However, you are much more likely to be appreciated by others if you are open and honest with your work colleagues, rather than struggling on alone, trying to keep up and ultimately not producing work of the required standard. It is quite possible, for instance, that the person asking you to do something might not have appreciated how much you already have on your plate; and how can he plan his own workload properly if he gets no feedback from you on whether what he is asking is reasonable or not?

By struggling on and then not managing to cope, you are much more likely to cause others to get angry with you – so the whole point of caving in to the original request backfires dramatically. So by not saying 'no', you can easily shoot yourself in the foot and actually become inefficient and late in your work – and ultimately overtired and unable to cope at all.

Now think of it the other way around. By being assertive
and explaining that you cannot take on yet another piece of
work, you are more likely to gain the respect of others and
also to allow them to understand that there is a physical
limitation that everyone comes up against in being able to
cope with all that is thrown at them.

There is also the question of self-respect. Those who fail to
produce quality work – regardless of whether it is 'their
fault' or not – often end up with a low estimation of
themselves. If, on top of that, they realise that by having
the courage to stand up for themselves they could have
avoided the situation in the first place, they are likely to
feel doubly dejected.

Of course, if others perceive you to be someone who has
little self-respect, they will begin to start treating you in that
way, and any negative feelings towards you could intensify.
At the opposite end of the scale, if others see you as being a
positive person, then that is how they will react to you.

The problem that many find extremely difficult is just how to say 'no' – especially to a superior member of staff. Doing so by making excuses is quite definitely not the way to do it. Apart from the fact that these excuses can either sound very lame, or be seen for what they are – telling downright lies – they are also highly likely to make the apologist feel nothing short of cowardly, which again is hardly likely to make him feel good about himself.

No, the only way you can say 'no' in this context is to be assertive. That does not mean that you have to be aggressive in your response; but by explaining why you cannot or will not do something someone has asked you, you may well find that it actually clears the air, rather than making the situation more difficult.

Of course, you will want to have convinced yourself first of all that what is being requested of you is something that you do not want to do. It may even be that you will need to ask for further details before you make up your mind. But it is much better to refuse at the outset once your mind is made up, rather than let it fester in the background.

It often helps to give a good reason why you do not wish to carry out a particular request. This does not mean that you should hand out a string of excuses. The person whose request you are refusing will respect you much more if you quietly, but firmly, explain your reasons for refusal, keeping your emotions firmly under control.

Finally, if you really do want to help the other person, but are unable to do so for whatever reason, it can do no harm to ask him if there is any way you can help him to find another solution to his problem.

Saying 'no' to one's boss or work colleagues is one thing. Saying 'no' to a customer or client is quite a different matter. Being on the front line, representing the company can often be quite a stressful experience. We all know the expression 'The customer is always right', but in reality it can be quite galling having to deal with difficult clients.

All of us are clients or customers, and we all appreciate being shown courtesy and consideration. It follows that many clients who may appear angry or aggressive often do so as a result of what they regard as poor service, or of being treated badly by the company in question.

Yet good customer service is important in dealing with the clients of any company, regardless of whether you work in a service industry or in manufacturing. Put yourself in your clients' shoes and ask yourself how you would respond in their situation. If they have encountered bad or inefficient service, don't they have a right to complain? And if they do feel that way about the company, then to whom are they going to make their feelings known? Why, to you, the front-line staff of course. So there really is no point in taking their abuse personally.

Often, it is extremely stressful to be harangued by an angry client. Keeping calm really is the only way to deal with such people because if you become irate as a result of how he talks to you, then absolutely nothing will be achieved, and his current perceptions of you and your company will only be reinforced. The logical consequence of this is that he may never come back for a second time, and worse still, he may bad-mouth your company to all his friends, thus ensuring that they never use your services either.

People don't get angry for no reason, and dissatisfied clients are usually angry for only a small number of possible reasons. Perhaps they feel:

- no-one appears to want to listen to them, or to take their complaints seriously
- the product they purchased does not work in the way it should
- they are not getting the help they require
- their expectations have not been met
- their complaint is not taken as seriously by the company as it is by them

In all of these cases, it is necessary to show them that you take what they are saying seriously. And that means listening, and showing them that you are not only listening but also taking notice. Take time to take in a few deep breaths, and try to relax your posture. If you are tensed up, you can never hide that fact from the other person.

Body language is very useful in this situation, as is paraphrasing what they have said to show that you have absorbed the essence of their concerns. By asking questions to learn more about their complaint, you would get to the heart of the problem more quickly.

In dealing with angry clients, you should also attempt to empathise with them. At the start of your conversation, you are unlikely to know if they have good cause to be upset. Try putting yourself in their position, listening carefully, maintaining eye contact and generally getting on the same wavelength so that you can demonstrate to them that there really is no question of it being a situation of them against your company, but rather that you are on their side to try to get things sorted out.

Once you have dealt with getting their feelings back on an even keel, you should set about dealing with the problem itself. One of the most powerful things anyone can do in such a situation is to ask directly 'What can I do to help?' However, it is no good then turning around and saying you cannot solve the problem. At the very least you will need to offer some alternatives so that at least you are seen to be making the effort to get somewhere close to resolving their problem.

Give your client at least two alternative solutions so that in effect you are giving him the option of taking control of the solution once again. Sometimes there may be no options for you even to offer, in which case you should explain why it is impossible to accede to his wishes. However, you should still do all you can to come up with some acceptable solution so that he can see that you are genuinely trying to help, and not to give him the brush-off.

The last thing you should do is to offer excuses as to why something has not been done. Frankly, the customer does not wish to know whose fault it was. As far as he is concerned, you are the public face of the company and it is the company that is at fault; therefore, by a logical extension, you are at fault. The most important thing is to get whatever was wrong put right. Once you have decided what must be done, explain what you intend to him and then make sure that you actually do it.

In summary, then:

- As soon as it becomes obvious that you will have to deal with a client who has a complaint, take a few deep breaths and try to relax yourself as much as possible
- Remain calm at all times and take an assertive stance, showing him that you are unfazed by his temper
- Try to see the situation from his point of view and empathise wherever possible with his predicament
- Listen, question and paraphrase wherever possible in order to demonstrate that you really do understand what his problems are
- Find out what, if any, his solution would be to the problem
- Offer a solution – if at all possible, incorporate his suggestions; but if not, attempt to create a solution acceptable to both parties

Complaints over the telephone can add further complications to finding a solution, for it is an unfortunate fact that many people, who would not dream of being rude to anyone directly, become much more aggressive where no facial contact is taking place. And because there is no non-verbal feedback going on – i.e. the facial expressions and the hand movements that we all take for granted in normal conversation – some people are altogether less coherent when talking over a phone.

How many times, also, have you been put on hold for an eternity by a not-very-bright receptionist and then put through to someone who is unable to help you anyway? It happens to all of us, and the worst part about it is not knowing what is happening at the other end of the line. Have they forgotten us? Do they care? Does anyone want to help us solve the problem? Would we be better off taking our business elsewhere?

So dealing with complainants over the telephone can often become even more stressful than facing the wrath of a difficult customer eyeball to eyeball. But equally, it is even more essential that you remain cool, calm and collected when dealing with such a person over the wires. Without the feedback inherent in body language, it is very important to give verbal feedback to the complainant that you are not only still listening to him, but also understand his problems and wish to help him find a solution to them.

When dealing with a difficult person over the telephone, you should:

- always ensure you have a notepad beside you so that you can note down his complaints; there could be more than one, after all!
- make sure that if you cannot help him to find a solution there and then, you will tell him that you will get back to him at a later time – and make sure you do!
- explain fully if you are unable to resolve his problem yourself, and that you will ask the relevant person to ring him back
- make sure that you have all his relevant details – his name, telephone number and address, and the reason why he called you in the first place

Unfortunately, there are sometimes occasions when the level of frustration or anger of the client reaches boiling point and he starts to swear or exhibit threatening behaviour. What should you do in such circumstances? There is a school of thought that says that no-one should have to put up with threatening or abusive language, and that in such a situation you should either put the phone down on the complainant or, in a person-to-person situation, simply walk away. Unfortunately, life is not that easy. There are quite a few scenarios, such as dealing with patients and their relatives in hospitals, where it would obviously be quite inappropriate to absolve oneself of their problems when they are emotionally charged up. Equally, however, no-one should normally have to be on the receiving end of such behaviour, and it is best if you are likely to find yourself in such a position that you discuss what is the company's policy on such matters before it actually happens.

It could also be a very good idea to see what it is that is making the clients unhappy with your service. Have you, for instance, given them expectations that cannot be met? Is the competition giving better service or better-quality products for the same price? If so, a proper review of your place in the market may well reduce the number of 'difficult people' you have to deal with altogether.

Summary

This Friday we have discussed the difficulties faced by many in having to say 'no' to a request, and to fend off unwarranted abuse from a difficult client.

- Do you have difficulty in saying 'no' to someone in authority?
- What is it that 'gets in the way' of your standing up to him?

- How do you intend to tackle him in the future if you find yourself in such a situation once again?

At the end of the day, dealing with such people is part of the job itself, and if you are easily offended or intimidated and feel you are unable to handle it, then maybe you should be doing something else for a living!

You're in control now

In going on this journey through the past week, it will have become clear to you that truly assertive behaviour is the most positive and productive way forward – the most likely to succeed, both for you and for the people around you. It is also the least likely to turn *you* into a difficult person.

If we look back to Monday, and the general definitions of the three basic character types, we see that assertiveness means being able to act without anxiety or fear, whilst expressing your needs and preferences without behaving in a threatening manner to others. It is the positive attitude toward the whole of the work and human relationships that can make the world go round, rather than punctuating life with a series of Mexican stand-offs or even a complete stalemate and abandonment of the plans and relationships involved.

As part of understanding that attitude, you have first to get to grips with understanding yourself and learning how to amend your behaviour and reactions to enable you to interact and work more effectively with others. Whatever your role in life, your understanding of where other people are coming from and why they are taking the stance they are, takes you more than halfway to being able to dynamise your relationship with them and improve it in so many ways. If you apply this philosophy in your workplace as well, you will enable your colleagues to work with you much more effectively.

The first step, then, is to understand yourself, however uncomfortable that may make you feel. After all, coming face to face with yourself is not always a pleasure; stick at it and make sure that you are not deluding yourself about any aspect of your own behaviour. You'll probably like yourself better afterwards too!

We have all seen friends and acquaintances deluding themselves on a daily basis, such as when:

- they only tell 'white' lies when they amend their CVs in order to change the substance of their recorded personal history
- they think that they are quiet, shy and retiring, when they are truly gregarious and tend to show off!
- they say they are 'on a diet' when, in reality, they snack all day

We are usually our own worst enemies in life anyway, and we are always sad to see friends who labour away under a damaging false premise - but how many of us are actually brave enough to grasp the nettle and tell them? Indeed, should we tell them at all?

It is a truism that many of us are the products of our own upbringing. We saw on Tuesday that although there are many different types of personality trait, the four main categories can be broken down into *insecure, negative, selfish* and *pleasant*. We would all like to see ourselves in the fourth camp, but in reality:

- how do others see us?
- how can we find out truthfully how others see us?
- has the insecurity of childhood left its scar on us for life?
- how much of that scar can we overcome in its negativity?
- have we really learned that others have needs too?
- do we take these into account when we are planning and speaking to others?
- can we better ourselves and help others with similar problems?
- how can we best develop ourselves to do that?

Then the knottiest problem of all – why are particular people a problem to us anyway? What is it that they do or say that really gets our goat? Am *I* the real problem here after all?

You need to ask these questions – or slightly milder versions of them – whenever a new situation arises or a potential conflict scenario appears to be looming up to overshadow your relationships and work.

Conflict is the spice of life and arises in all kinds of everyday situations, but it has to be stressed that not all conflict is bad. Your managing the conflict in your life is the key to avoiding stress, and so the perception of what it is that is causing the conflict in the first place is well worth achieving. Put succinctly, conflict can be either positive or negative. By positive conflict, we are referring to a situation in which the generation of enthusiasm can be the catalyst to solving a problem that up till now has remained stubbornly impenetrable. Negative conflict, on the other hand, can lead both to stress and to the failure of the two parties to come to any kind of agreement.

The key is to find common ground and attempt to see things from the other person's point of view. That doesn't necessarily mean he is right; only that his opinion should not be dismissed out of hand: for it is perfectly possible to see things from a number of different angles, each one of which may well be valid. We all know the story of the three blind men stumbling across an elephant. One came across its trunk, whilst the second was fanned by one of its ears. The third walked into one of its massive legs. Who gave the best description of this animal? Would the blind man who described a snake-like creature be any more wrong – or right – than one of his colleagues who had experienced a downdraught from a giant fan, or the other who thought he had discovered a giant tree trunk?

Being negative and putting a dampener on things is all too easy. Everyone gets depressed at times, but inevitably it is the positive people in society who get things moving and who win in the end. So if in addition to being positive in your own right, you get others to behave positively to you too, then it follows that you are much more likely to find a way forward in all aspects of your life.

But what do we mean by being positive? It certainly is not the same as being a 'yes' person. Being positive means looking for a way forward through a difficult situation, looking for the good things and working out how to improve the bad. Sometimes that is simply a matter of improving your communications skills in order to give feedback to your opposite number. Being able to interpret non-verbal signals and to back up your own conversation with body language are also skills that are well worth developing in order to avoid misunderstandings.

Equally, many people experience great difficulty when finding themselves in a situation where they have to say 'no' to someone. We none of us like doing it, because it is against basic human nature. But being able to say 'no' is an important weapon in our armoury of techniques for being more open and honest with our colleagues. It isn't easy; no-one ever said it was. But by tackling the difficult situation head-on, you are less likely to store up further problems in the future, and equally you will end up better respected by your colleagues who will see you as a straight-dealing type of guy to be working with!

At the end of the day, good communication is at the very heart of dealing with difficult people. Many people can be exasperating, and there are times when we all wonder if there is any point in putting up with their general behaviour and attitudes. Yet, give in to the temptation of treating like with like and who wins in the end? You don't, because you will soon see that by behaving like your opposite number you have actually sunk to his level. He doesn't either, because for a start he has lost your respect and most likely the respect of others around you. It is worth remembering there is an old adage which goes something along the lines of 'When you point an accusing finger at somebody you should watch out as there are always three fingers that are pointing back at you'! Without sounding awfully 'goody goody', assertive behaviour and setting a good example can be an inspiration to others. On the other hand, following their lead and behaving badly, giving others a difficult time, can never lead to a positive outcome. Perhaps Charles Kingsley, in his famous tome *The Water Babies*, summed up the situation perfectly with his two characters Mrs 'Do-as-you-would-be-done-by' and Mrs 'Be-done-by-as-you-did'.

So get positive, try to see the other person's point of view and, above all, communicate, and hopefully other people will soon stop being difficult in your company and will perhaps surprise even themselves. Surely that has to be a good thing?

Summary

The keys to dealing with difficult people can be found within ourselves. Over the past week, we have found ourselves turning full circle until we see a mirror image of ourselves in others. It is only when we can control our own behaviour and see the potential reactions of others more clearly that we can even hope to begin the process of enabling them to react differently. This way we can all learn to deal with difficult people – who may then suddenly start to become less difficult!

Further *Successful Business in a Week* **titles all at £6.99.** A complete listing of all titles can be obtained from Katie Ingram on 0171 873 6261.

All Hodder & Stoughton books are available from your local bookshop or can be ordered direct from the publisher. Just tick the titles you want and fill in the form below. Prices and availability subject to change without notice.

To: Hodder & Stoughton Ltd, Cash Sales Department, Bookpoint, 39 Milton Park, Abingdon, Oxon, OX14 4TD. If you have a credit card you may order by telephone – 01235 400414.

E-mail address: orders@bookpoint.co.uk

Please enclose a cheque or postal order made payable to Bookpoint Ltd to the value of the cover price and allow the following for postage and packaging:

UK & BFPO: £1.00 for the first book, 50p for the second book and 30p for each additional book ordered up to a maximum charge of £3.00.

OVERSEAS & EIRE: £2.00 for the first book, £1.00 for the second book and 50p for each additional book.

Name: ....

Address: ....

....

If you would prefer to pay by credit card, please complete:

Please debit my Visa/Mastercard/Diner's Card/American Express (delete as appropriate) card no:

❏ ❏ ❏ ❏ ❏ ❏ ❏ ❏ ❏ ❏ ❏ ❏ ❏ ❏ ❏ ❏

Signature .... Expiry Date ....